The Only Debt Guide You Need

Getting you out of debt in 20 pages

Jared Allegretta

Copyright © 2018 Jared Allegretta

All rights reserved.

ISBN:1987726340
ISBN-13: **978-1987726343**

DEDICATION

To my Wife who was willing to ignore and endure all of my financial hacking and experiments.

Thank you.

CONTENTS

	What is this book?	i
1	We can fix this	Pg 1
2	What do you owe?	Pg 4
3	What do you earn?	Pg 5
4	Min Maxing	Pg 7
5	Payback	Pg 9
6	Kickstart the process	Pg 12
7	What do I do next?	Pg 15
8	Resources	Pg 16

WHAT IS THIS BOOK?

I wrote this guide as a simple and straight forward teaching tool. Most people are in debt of some kind and don't know how to get out. It can seem nearly impossible to be debt free and even the idea of it seems like a pipe dream or scheme of some sort.
That's how screwed up we are, not owing money seems weird to us.
Debt should not be the norm and it really doesn't have to be. I've spent years learning about personal finance and I've boiled it down to this. A simple and realistic step by step guide to get and stay out of debt. If you follow the steps here and commit to them you can dig yourself out of the hole in a few years instead of never.
This is not a magic trick. This will not be fast, or easy but it will work if you can commit to it.

This guide is designed to skip all the theory and fluff. For the most part I'm not describing the mechanics or reasoning behind what we are doing, instead we are stripping away all we can and just getting down to brass tacks. This isn't a book designed to teach you about person finance, it's designed to get you out of debt and keep you there.

The deeper understanding of these topics IS important, but we'll save it for another time. Let's get you going.

1. We Can Fix This

Being in debt sucks. Flat out that's the best way to say it. If you owe money it can have a whole host of effects on you, more than most people understand. There's the obvious effects like not being able to pay your bills, collection calls, never being able to afford anything you want and sometimes the things you need. Beside that comes the constant stress and worry, your social life takes a hit because you can't afford to go out and then there's that always present feeling of shame or failure following you around. It eats at you little by little in the back of your head causing you to have to "just not care" anymore. That of course allows you to justify the next purchase you clearly shouldn't make because hey "I'm already in debt, what's another $30". This is one of the ways that debt begets debt, it gets in your head.

Holding debt on your ledger will create more debt over time. Aside from the mental effects and bad decisions it can bring, think about your bank. If you make a debit purchase of $10.00 but had $9.99 in your bank account you'll overdraft $0. 01....and get charged a $30 fee.

Another common scenario is getting a speeding ticket. You wind up late to work and drive a little fast to avoid losing money then you get pulled over for speeding and ticketed $200. You miss that shift, AND now you owe money. You don't have $200, so they charge you late fees increasing the amount owed. Every time you don't pay it on time because you CAN'T it increases again to make sure you REALLY can't. Then one day you either get your license suspended, car impounded, jail time or if you're lucky, all the above. It spirals quickly.

Scenario three, borrowing money. If you have need for a loan, let's say to pay a speeding ticket, you get charged interest. If you are wealthy and able to pay your bills you have good credit and pay little to no interest. If you are middle or lower class you obviously have a much higher change of having poor credit, which makes borrowing money and taking credit carry a much higher interest rate. It makes sense for the creditor don't get me wrong, but again it penalizes people without money by making things more expensive for them.

Money creates money and debt creates debt

So yeah, debt sucks. But it's not insurmountable and it can be managed and defeated much easier than you think. It won't cost you money for classes and you don't have to pay anyone to help negotiate it away. You can do it on your own, in as little or as much time as you want. I'll show you how to do it and while we're at it I'll change how you think of money all together. In fact, that's the first lesson.

Money isn't what you think. It's not real and has no value. This is the first lesson you need to learn before you can get anywhere financially. Money is nothing but a tool to be used to get you what you want and need. It is not value, it buys value.

Here is what we are going to do:

1 - Redefine a few terms

2 - Organize your finances

3 - Develop a plan to pay it off.

4 - Work on speeding it up a bit

5 – Point you where to go next

To get yourself out of a hole, you first have to know how deep it is and what material the ground is made of. There's some more analogy there somewhere but let's skip it and move on to the important stuff.

2. What do you owe?

You need to know the difference between expenses and liabilities and how much of each you have.

We are going to ignore the dictionary here, I encourage you to know the real definition of each but for today's purposes we have our own. I want you to think of expenses as your normal monthly bills that can be cancelled. Phone, cable, internet, heat, basically any service. What we are going to consider a liability is anything you owe that can't be cancelled. Here I mean things like loans, credit card debt, car payments...borrowed money with a balance. The only thing I consider an expense that is actually a liability is a mortgage payment, as it can normally only be replaced by another expense, rent.

Go collect all your bills and include anything you owe anyone from all of time and space. Begin filling out an expense sheet (on the last pages) with the monthly payment, balances, and interest rates. We are going to use this sheet a lot so be thorough and honest.

Skip the part about income for now, we are going over that in the next section. Go do this before moving on to chapter 3.

3. What do you earn?

The next set of terms I want you familiar with are income, assets and passive.

Again, we are going to abandon Webster here and think of them in our own way. Income will be considered anything you work for. It's your paycheck. An asset is anything other than work that when owned produces money. Consider things like rental properties or certificates of deposit from the bank. Passive income is the income produced with little or no effort, it's what assets produce.

One major difference between the rich and poor is in how they buy things. Poor people use money to purchase things, rich people use money to purchase assets and let the assets purchase things. If I buy a $200 computer with a paycheck I have a computer and I'm out $200. If I buy a $1000 asset and let it pay out $200 over time then use that to buy the computer, I have a computer AND a $1000 asset that can keep buying things.

You should fill out the part of the sheet that asks for income **now**.

With the sheet filled out you should now have a pretty good idea of your financial position. Is it better or worse than you thought? Never mind that, the important thing is you know and armed with this knowledge we can make a plan that works for you. You know how much money is coming in, going out and most importantly what it's paying for.

Hold on to the sheet for later, because first we have some work to do.

The next bit seems obvious but humor me and actually do the damn work. Chapter 4 is about minimizing money going out and maximizing money coming in. This is part of preparing for Chapter 5.

4. Min Maxing

Now that we have your cash flow figured out we want to make it as efficient as possible. That will allow us to crush your liabilities faster. We are going to take this opportunity to minimize your expenses and maximize your income.

Let's start with minimizing. We are going to have to practice some reductionism here, if you want to get ahead there will be some sacrifices. Now I'm not one of those crazy people telling you to live on a shoestring and buy store brand toilet paper, that's just not what I'm about. What I will say is that different people are comfortable making different levels of sacrifice for this cause and that's okay. You don't have to feel bad that you aren't going to give up everything you enjoy in life to get out of debt, you can still have that Mocha Frappuccino latte. Just understand that the harder the lifestyle change you make now toward saving and reducing the faster you will reach your goals. If you want to take it easy that's fine too, your timeframe is your own.

Start by cutting your expense line. This may be hard for some people but really you should be able to trim at least some if not a whole lot out. Maybe it's less entertainment, maybe it's carpooling to save gas, maybe it's bringing lunch to work instead of buying it every day. You could cut the cord on cable or reduce your data plan. You may find that it's time to downsize to a smaller or cheaper apartment or get a roommate. You may also want to sell things you don't need or that cost you money.

One thing you should never overlook is negotiating your bills. You can call around for better insurance rates, cable TV bills, cell phone plans even interest rates on credit cards.

There are always things to cut, I'll let you figure that part out on your own. There are a lot of great resources for that sort of thing and you should research them all. You can use a program like **Trim** to help you.

After you reduce some expenses we must look at your income. It sounds obvious but it's often overlooked. This is straight forward though, ask for a raise or apply for a better paying job. Sometimes applying for a new job that pays a little more will prompt your company to match it to keep you.

You should ask, if you don't there's a 100% chance you won't get it. If they can't or won't do it, look for something better. In fact, you should ALWAYS be looking for something better, the best time to find a job is when you already have one.

The second obvious thing, get a part time job too. This is part of that sacrifice thing I was talking about earlier. It sucks to work multiple jobs but look at your liability total and imagine an extra $250 a week being applied to it…. it's a huge difference. Also it can be temporary.

If you followed these steps you have now reduced your expenses and increased your income. If you reduce your expenses by $100 and earn an additional $250 you can apply $350 more a month to your debts. Again, the more you sacrifice here the faster you will be debt free. You don't have to finish this step before the payback begins, but it's a good idea to at least get it started. Yeah this all seems obvious but then why haven't you already done it?

5. Payback

This is a long-used approach and there is a ton of material out there on it. I'll make it as straight forward as possible. The first thing you need to do is create your hit list, what debts will you go after first?

Method #1 - Save the most money (Avalanche method)

Go through each bill and write down the minimum payment due and the finance charge from the previous month. Compare the 4 finance charges to determine what card is costing you the most money each month. Rank them in order of most to least expensive and you just created your payoff list.

Method #2 - Quickest payoff possible (Snowball method)

Ignore the interest rate and just write down the minimum payment and balance of each card. Rank them from least to most.

Regardless of which way you choose to create your hit list, once you have it you can move on to the next step. I like to choose method 2 because when dealing with the phycological burden of debt a quick win can keep you on the right track. People like to win, and they are more likely to not give up on something they are succeeding at.

Let's make up a scenario using method 2 where you have 4 credit cards holding debt of $6700 total:

Creditor	Minimum payment	balance
Card 1 -	25	1200
Card 2 -	35	1500
Card 3 -	40	1800
Card 4 -	50	2200

For our example let's say you made it through the Min Max step and can free up an extra $50 a month to pay bills. So, at first $50 is our snowball.

Go ahead and pay all your normal bills including the minimum payments for each card. Then throw the extra $50 at card number 1. From this point you will be paying at least $75 toward this card which should have you paid back in about 18 months. Obviously, you will now pay it off much faster because you are going to focus everything you have on it. This card, though small, is your biggest hurdle. Right now, you have the least amount of resources you will ever have making it very tough. Also 18 months for your first zero balance seems like it will take forever but don't fret, we have ways to speed up the process.

After the First card is at a zero balance we take the snowball, $50 and add the minimum payment from card 1 which was $25, to give us a new snowball of $75. Then we move to the next card and repeat the process. Now we will add $75 to the $35 minimum payment on card 2 and we are paying $110. The second card here would be paid off in about 14 months.

The third card would be paid $150 and be gone in 12 months and the fourth card would be paid $200 and gone in about 12 months.

This is a worst-case scenario of 4 years to pay off the debts. This is without taking any other actions to lower them and not paying any extra when you can. 4 years is a lot better than the 70 it would take with minimum payments don't you think?

But here in America we don't like waiting, we want results fast. Next, we will go over a list of things you can do to speed the process along.

Why is it called the snowball method?

Think about Bugs Bunny tossing a snowball downhill toward Elmer Fudd. As it rolls down it gathers more and more snow, before it hits him it's a huge boulder. You're doing that to you debts.

Auto pilot and avoid late fees:

Automate your income and bills with direct deposit

and scheduled online bill payments. Set alerts on

your phone or computer to remind you to check up on

it once a month and to make your extra payments.

6. Kickstart the process

Let's assume you are highly motivated and want to move this along as fast as you can. In that case you know what you must do. Let's go over a few things you can do to speed up the process and build that snowball.

Sell your stuff

I have written articles about this before but I think it's often ignored. Selling your old things can net you a hefty sum and at the same time help reduce stress, clutter and some debt. Have a garage sale, Sell things on Amazon, eBay, Letgo or any number of apps. Imagine taking a weekend to do this and knocking $500 off your first card the next day.

Work part time

Even if it's only a day or two each week. Even if the work is degrading for you. You could get a part time job at Home Depot making $11 an hour and work 3 nights a week. That can be a take home of $800 a month and knock out the first card in under two months. Also, the more you work the less you can spend, just remember to pack a lunch so your expenses don't go up.

Credit Arbitrage

You can move debt around from cards with high interest to ones with lower rates. This can help reduce the rate at which you accumulate debt and that helps you pay it back faster. Just be careful of the fees that can go along with it, they could erase your progress. You can also try taking out consolidation loans and moving your debt to fewer places. The more spread out you are the harder it is to focus fire; your money is strongest in one place.

Negotiate

Call your card providers and politely ask if they can lower your interest rates. Tell them you are trying to get yourself out of debt and if they can do anything you would appreciate it. Some companies will lower your rate just for asking. If they say no ask for a reason, so that you have a goal to work toward. Do NOT let them talk you into a new card or changing programs. Once you clear the first card out you can call them back, this time with leverage. Having a zero balance gives you a stronger hand in your ask, they know you can just cancel if they don't play ball.

Earn some passive income

You can use programs like Inbox Dollars to earn a few bucks with very little effort. I bring in about $30 a month using it just for letting some ads run on my phone. There is a lot of potential in this sort of thing. Passive income will become a big part of your future after you get rid of these debts. It's good to start some of these lesser or entry level programs now to learn about them.

Read and Research

You should always be on the lookout for books about financial literacy. Read a book or a few articles online every month for ideas and inspiration. The most important thing going forward is that you need to always be increasing your financial IQ. You don't have to spend big bucks here either, buy used paperback editions from auction sites and pay pennies on the dollar for books on Personal Finance.

Google

Did he just tell me to Google it? Yes, Yes he did. There are going to be thousands of websites and booksellers out there all wanting to teach you how to handle your finances. As long as they aren't asking you for money first, read them all. No one person is going to know all of it or be 100% accurate for that matter. Again always be reading, always be learning and always (DYOR) Do Your Own Research .

7. What do I do next?

This is only the beginning of your journey. Once you find yourself debt free your possibilities are going to be wide open. During this process you will learn self-control, planning and patience all of which are the keys to making you wealthy.

With these skills and knowledge you are going to be able to research and plan for your retirement and then your EARLY retirement.

Now is the time to evaluate what you want out of life and set financial goals you need to get there. Most importantly I want you to commit to yourself that you will continue to learn all you can about personal finance and never stop. Time is on your side and will amplify your efforts of you continue down the right financial path.

Your next step is to work out your short and long term goals. These should consist of tax advantaged accounts, additional streams of income, investing and passive income. Use the resources in the end of this book to get a start and don't forget to revisit this book every few years to keep you on track.

Good luck out there.

8. Resources

Web sites to learn from:

The first few are sites from writers in Personal Finance. These are important to read because they give a perspective of regular people that started with nothing and learned their way up.

I have also added a few large companies sites because we can't ignore what's worked in the past. At its heart the rules of finance are the same from the little guy to the top. You should strive to understand all perspectives on finance to be successful.

www.Jallegretta.com/PersonalFinance

This is my personal site. You will find much more detailed explanations of these topics and more. I tend to write in a conversational manner and from experience.

www.Thesimpledollar.com

Trent Hamm is a great resource and I've followed him for years. He has multiple writers now and give some great advice.

www.iwillteachyoutoberich.com

Ramit Sethi has developed an entire brand around being successful. His site still holds a boat load of useful information in his blog section.

www.Kiplinger.com

These folks are a more traditional company and perspective. I find their site intuitive and informative. They include more market and business news.

www.Marketwatch.com

Published by Dow Jones & Co. Strictly info on the greater economy. The articles are written at an easy to digest level so you don't need to understand everything about global to find it useful. This site can teach you a lot about the US economy.

Lastly I want you to go to Google and type in "Personal Finance Blogs"

See what comes up. There are thousands of sites dedicated to teaching you these things. Each with a unique perspective. I encourage you to find the ones that speak to you and help you, even if they aren't mine.

Recommended reading:

There are several books that started most of us on this journey. For some people they are the same few. Here are a few I think make good reading.

Rich Dad Poor Dad

The first real finance book I read. It taught me a lot, not about how to earn money but how to think about money. This book can change your viewpoint and it's worth it just for that. I would personally avoid trying to follow any of the actual methods for gain, they are super risky.

The 4 Hour Workweek

This book blew the doors off finance for me. I still read this one every year or two to refresh myself. Tim Ferris actually shows you how to do specific things in this one and how he talks about finance is life altering.

Your Money or Your Life

One of the first true to form Personal Finance books of the modern age. This book goes deep into your personal values, integrity, life goals…it gets pretty personal. Consider this one a 12 step program for your finances but in 9 steps.

A list of useful Apps and sites to manage and invest.

www.Mint.com

Purchased by Intuit, this site can track all of your finances for you and digest it into readable actionable info. Pie charts, budgets, projections and so much more. I use it as a backup to my normal record keeping.

www.Bankrate.com

These guys have a few services but moat useful are their financial calculators.

Acorns

A phone app designed to round up your purchases to the nearest dollar and invest that money for you. It's a great way to force a little earnings $5 at a time.

Betterment

Another investing app and website for investing. This is a bit more serious and larger in scope but they help choosing funds based on your goals. Your portfolio is manageable from your phone.

Stash

Similar to Betterment, this one focuses more on teaching and investing is based on values based investing. You can choose funds that are environmentally friendly, focus on social media or based on travel. More options in general can be found here.

Also important is whatever app your bank uses. You want to have control over your finances and accounts at all times and that's the best way to do it.

The following sheet is designed as a template for you to start tracking your finances. Add all of your monthly expenses to it and fill it in as completely as you possibly can. As stated earlier the more thorough you are here the better your outcome will be. If you need more space, recreate this in Excel or Google docs.

Don't forget to go through your bank statements, that pile of bills on the table over there and your online accounts. Add your income after taxes and deductions, what you take home.

If you have other bills that aren't monthly try to average them out to come up with a monthly estimate.

When you complete this sheet the difference between your income and expenses is what you can afford to spend and will be the basis to determine your starting snowball size.

Expense	Monthly		Income	
Mortgage/rent			Expenses	
Electric			Difference	
Heat				
Phone				
Internet				
Car Insurance				
Gas				
Food				
Entertainment				

Liability	Monthly	Balance	Interest rate	Interest cost

ABOUT THE AUTHOR

I spent most of my youth being poor. I mean like waiting on line for government cheese poor. For a time, I was homeless. It was sometime in my early 20's that I decided that had to change, I wasn't quite sure how but I was determined to fix it. When trying to come up with a realistic plan to get out of debt and start moving up the financial ladder I thought I'll need to start at the beginning, so I went to Google and typed in "What is money?".

That was the start of what has become a lifelong lesson.

As I normally do I went overboard and got a little obsessed with the topic, now known to me as Personal Finance. I spent years on end studying it and moved my career into finance. I got my License for Life, Accident and Health Insurance and years later began working in a bank, I wanted to know money from every angle. I even studied for the series 6 and 7 exams to be a stock broker. In 2008 I began blogging at Personal Finance Spotlight and I've maintained it on and off ever since.

I went to school for Retail Management for a few years before changing Majors to Computer Programming. I left the bank and let my licenses expire. I did not pursue trading as a career. Me and sales, turns out we don't get along.

I am not a salesman. I don't like asking people to spend money on things I don't think they need. I got into personal finance to help people save and earn more money, not spend it. So here I am trying to do just that. I spent 10 years getting myself to the point I'm at today and I'd like to help other people do the same. Everyone deserves the chance to be financially stable, no matter what you were born into to.

www.ingramcontent.com/pod-product-compliance
Lightning Source LLC
Chambersburg PA
CBHW032311240526
45464CB00023BA/2989